CEDRIC'S BUS'

The Adventures of Cedric the Spider

Written by

JACK WEBB

Illustrated by

GARY STOCKER

JACK WEBB

ISBN:
ISBN-13: 9781728662121

To Edward,

I hope you really enjoy reading about Cedric and his friends!

With very best wishes,

Jack Webb,

(John Player)

SEVEN BUSY NIGHTS

ACKNOWLEDGEMENTS

This book would never have been written and published without the help of the following:

My daughter Emily who initially inspired me to write down the Cedric stories for the children and grandchildren in our ever-growing family.

My son Edmund, who with Emily, provided the memories of Cedric stories told at bedtime when they were children, as well as new ideas and suggestions for the plot and characters.

Gary, whose wonderful illustrations have brought the book to life. His patience, advice and friendship have been indispensable in bringing the stories to print.

To my cats, Florence and Brian (sadly deceased) for allowing me to portray them so vividly.

Finally, to my dear wife Brenda, who has been such an encouragement and a faithful audience for the stories as they evolved.

MONDAY NIGHT - DOWN THE DRAIN

Cedric's busy week began in the bathroom of number 24, March Meadow, the semi-detached home of Mr and Mrs Evershed and their two children, Millie, aged 9, and Robert, 7, who everyone knew as Bobby.

The bathroom, of course, is the place for daily washing and brushing, bathing and showering, but also happened to be the home of Cedric the Spider. Well, sort of. Cedric lived down the bath plug hole but would emerge into the bottom of the bath when all was quiet and would slip silently back down the plug hole while the family was using the bathroom.

He liked his small, dark, cosy home and always enjoyed a shower himself when one of the family pulled the bath plug to let the water out.

It was late evening. Millie and Bobby had brushed their

teeth and were asleep in bed, while Mr and Mrs Evershed had just turned off their bedside lamps after a long day and a short read.

They then settled down to a good night's rest. All was quiet, but in the bathroom a faint rustle and some tiny voices could be heard.

"Hurry up, Belinda," whispered Bertie the toothbrush, impatiently beckoning his elder sister to jump out of the toothbrush rack, "but don't wake the grown-ups!" Bertie was smaller than Belinda, but had the same shiny white, angled bristles, though with a bright orange handle from the end of which protruded his tiny retractable legs, which, like his little arms, were, of course, invisible to their human owners. Belinda, a pleasantly pale purple young brush, jumped from the rack in her own good time and followed Bertie on one of their exciting nocturnal adventures. "I know," said Bertie. "Let's play sliding down the end of the bath towards the plug hole. The one who slides the furthest, wins, and if you rub some wet soap on your handle, you'll go further!" As everyone had used the soap at bedtime, it was still moist and provided the small toothbrushes with very effective skid lubrication. Down the bathtub they slid, with Bertie insisting on going first, but being easily outdistanced by Belinda who stopped just short of the plug, quietly smiling to herself.

"That's not fair!" shouted Bertie. "You cheated! You must have used more soap than me!"

"Typical boy. You never wash properly." Belinda replied, and a brother sister spat seemed inevitable, when, out of the darkness, a short, sharp voice called out "Do you two mind keeping quiet! I'm trying to get some rest down here." The two junior toothbrushes looked up, then behind them, then left, then right, but when their eyes looked down towards the plug hole, they were more than surprised to see a rather large, grumpy arachnid (that's a spider to you and me), staring at them with small, beady, bad-tempered eyes.

"Aaaaah!" shrieked both brushes, nearly waking the whole household and with bristles standing on end, "A spider!!!"

"Oh, don't be silly," said Cedric. "I wouldn't hurt a fly, let alone toothbrushes and humans. Well, that's not quite true," he continued. "I actually eat flies. They're my favourite food, but that's different and arises out of necessity."

"I didn't know spiders could talk," Bertie exclaimed and Belinda, sitting beside him, tilted her head in agreement.

"I expect there's a lot you don't know about spiders," Cedric declared. "One. We eat all those nasty indoor pests, like flies, moths and mosquitoes. Two. We help control germs which pests spread, causing human diseases. Three. We eat the bugs that destroy food crops. Four ...."

"Yes! O.K. You've made your point but ..."

"And I've got 8 legs. That's 4 times more than you have, although I confess I've never seen a walking toothbrush. Who are you and where do you come from?"

"My name is Belinda, and this is my brother Bertie.

We're the toothbrushes which the children, Millie and Bobby, use, and we live in the toothbrush rack above the bathroom sink."

"And what's *your* name?" enquired Bertie. "Where do *you* come from?"

"My name is Cedric Aloysius Octopod, but you can call me Cedric the Spider, although just Cedric will do nicely, and I happen to live in the vent pipe down the drain of your bath plug. It's cool, dry and safe, and a great place to spin my webs so I can store the flies I catch. Anyway, I don't know why I am telling you all this. Why don't you come and see for yourselves?"

"Do you think we should?" Belinda queried hesitantly, to which Bertie immediately replied "Of course we should!

Come on! Let's go …"

Cedric led the way into the plug hole followed by a very excited Bertie and a rather more cautious Belinda. The toothbrushes both had difficulty squeezing through one of the strainer holes, flattening their bristles and flexing their backs as their eyes gradually grew accustomed to the deepening darkness of the drain.

"Prepare yourselves for a soaking," called Cedric. "We're about to go through the water trap at the U-bend. Hold your breath. It's not long but you'll need to flex a bit."

"We don't mind water," Belinda declared. "We get two soakings every day when the children clean their teeth!"

Soon they were out of the water and feeling their way behind Cedric through a long drain tunnel with several junctions until they reached another bend, beyond which they began a long climb upwards.

Eventually the tunnel widened and levelled out, whereupon the two young toothbrushes felt a draught of fresh air and were surprised to see a faint shimmer of light.

"Here we are," said Cedric, "and may I introduce you to Lux and Lumen, the glow worm twins. They are my guests and provide free lighting in return for Bed & Breakfast. I suppose you might call them lightbulb lodgers. They keep themselves to themselves and live up there on the drain ceiling, but they certainly brighten up the place!"

"Hello!" said the toothbrushes, in an attempt to be polite and friendly.

"So," said Lux. "Like," said Lumen.

"Oh, don't bother trying to talk to them," Cedric interjected. "Although they can understand you, they only speak Larvin and it's a rather limited language with just two words."

"Like," said Lux. "So," said Lumen.

Sounds like Millie, Belinda thought to herself.

"Now, would you like to see my larder?" Cedric continued. "It's just along here."

They proceeded a little further along the drain up to a large network of interwoven spider webs, containing an assortment of lifeless bugs, flies and moths, dangling down from the ceiling in front of them.

"Uuuugh!" Belinda and Bertie looked at each other with an air of revulsion, even though their main purpose in life was to clean left-over food from Millie and Bobby's teeth!

"And this is my bed!" Cedric had moved on and pointed towards another broad, silky web fixed on opposite sides of the drain, which provided the cheery spider with a comfortable hammock along the lines of a trampoline.

"Wow!" exclaimed Bertie. "Can I bounce on it? I'll be careful."

"Well, you won't break it. Some people say that a spider web is stronger than steel, but that's not actually true. But take care; it's very springy."

With that, Bertie leapt up on to the web and proceeded to bounce energetically until he hit his head on the drain ceiling, fell awkwardly on to the side of the web, tripped over a supporting thread and tumbled heavily, at least for a toothbrush, on to the floor.

"Ouch," cried Bertie. "That hurt."

"You'll live." said Belinda, then added, chuckling to herself "You wanted to treat Cedric's bed as a trampoline and he did warn you. Anyway, you look funny; you've flattened the bristles on the top of your head!"

At this point Bertie, too, saw the funny side of his predicament and noticed that even Cedric was grinning.

"Can we go any further?" he asked. "Where do the pipes lead to? What's up there?"

"Slow down, young Bertie," replied Cedric. "There are plenty of adventures to be had, some up, some down and some outside. But they are all for another day. You two must be getting back to the bathroom or the grown-up toothbrushes will be wondering where you've gone, and it wouldn't do if you weren't there to brush Millie and Bobby's teeth in the morning now, would it?. Off you go!"

"You'll show us the way, won't you Cedric?" Belinda pleaded. "We'd get lost travelling along all those pipes on our own."

"I won't be coming with you," Cedric replied. "But don't worry. You'll get back all right."

"But how?!" they both exclaimed anxiously.

"You'll use the thread I spun on the way here. Hold on to it and it'll take you right back to the water trap. When you get there, just hold your breath, dive into the water, round the U bend, and you'll be back at the plug hole. Then, if you like and if you're brave enough, you can come here again tomorrow night and I'll show you what's at the end of one of the other tunnels."

"Really?" they both shouted in excitement.

Bertie couldn't believe his luck, "I'm brave enough," he declared, but Belinda hadn't forgotten her manners:

"Well, if you truly don't mind and if we're not taking up your time …"

"Certainly not, young lady. It's been a pleasure having some company. Lux and Lumen aren't exactly a laugh a minute and I've plenty of food in the larder so I don't need to go catching any more bugs until next week. I'll take you both to meet some old friends."

The two brushes bristled with enthusiasm, tempered slightly by the uneasy thought of making their way back down the drain on their own.

With that, the genial little spider sidled along the drain to his larder. The toothbrushes looked nervously at each other, then grabbed the guiding thread and made their way back the way they had come.

When they had gone down the vent pipe and entered the damper part of the drain, they suddenly heard a familiar flushing noise and then the sound of rushing water coming towards them!

Mr Evershed had had a very relaxing evening with his wife, watching a good film, and supping one or two glasses of wine, but nature had caught up with him in the night and he had woken well before daylight, feeling the need for a quick tiddle! "Must remember to buy the children some new toothbrushes," he thought to himself as he rinsed his hands at the sink noticing, with bleary eyes, two empty slots in the toothbrush rack. "God knows what they've done with them!"

"Run!" shouted Belinda, and the two brushes just managed to squeeze into a side drain as the flushed water rushed past.

"That was close!" squealed Bertie. "Why did he have to do that, tonight of all nights? Where are we?"

They both groped around in the dark for at least ten minutes until, at last, Belinda shouted with immense relief, "I've found it! I've found the guiding thread. Over here, Bertie!"

The two brushes grasped the thread and continued back towards the bath until, after what seemed a lifetime, they eventually reached the water trap. Taking a deep breath, they plunged into the water, negotiated the U bend and emerged just beneath the plug hole. Listening out for any noise or movement, they squeezed silently through one of the strainer holes and surfaced into the bottom of the bath. With difficulty and after two backward slides, they scrambled up the side of the bath and clambered along the shelf to the sink, where they had a quick rinse before getting back up to their rack and slipping quietly into their respective slots next to Mr and Mrs Evershed's toothbrushes, who themselves were dozing and seemingly unaware of Belinda and Bertie's exploits.

Mr Evershed rose at his usual time of 6 o'clock the following morning. Entering the bathroom for a quick shower and shave before breakfast, he stared fixedly at the toothbrush rack. "I could have sworn that there were only two toothbrushes in the rack when I got up in the night. How many glasses of wine DID I have …?

TUESDAY NIGHT - ON THE TILES

Bertie and Belinda, the toothbrushes belonging to Bobby and Millie Evershed, were terribly excited. They were going on an adventure with Cedric the Spider, whose full name was Cedric Aloysius Octopod, and who lived in the drain below the Evershed's bath plug. Mrs Evershed had just finished in the bathroom and gone into the bedroom where Mr Evershed was having a read - a newspaper article about the dangers of drinking too much wine. Millie and Bobby were fast asleep in their beds and it wasn't long before their parents had switched off their reading lamps and joined their children in the land of nod.

Bertie, an orange toothbrush for children aged 5 – 7, prodded his sister Belinda who was resting in the slot beside him in the toothbrush rack.

"Time to go!" he whispered.

Belinda, pale purple and suitable for children aged 8 -11, jumped out of her slot and followed Bertie to the sink, along the shelf and down into the bath. When they reached the plug hole, they looked nervously at each other.

"I hope that the guiding thread hasn't been washed away," said Belinda. "We should never be able to find our way to Cedric's home without it."

"There's only one way to find out!" Bertie exclaimed and, flexing his back, he squeezed through one of the strainer holes and down into the drain. Belinda, not wanting to be left behind and always conscious of her duty to look after her rather impetuous younger brother, followed on quickly behind.

Next, they held their breath as they plunged into the water trap, round the U bend, and out into the gloom of the drain itself. They both felt the wall all around them until Bertie, with a delighted cry of "Yes!", found the guiding thread, a long, single strand of spider web spun by Cedric to signpost the way to his home in the air vent. Steadily upwards and across, and it wasn't too long before they began to feel the fresh air in the vent and saw the glimmer of light formed by the twin glow worms, Lux and Lumen, the lightbulb lodgers who lived on the drain ceiling above Cedric's cosy dwelling.

"Up or down?" The brushes heard the familiar, cheery voice of Cedric, who had emerged from his webby larder munching the remains of a housefly. "Do you want to go up the air vent or down the soil stack?"

"What's the difference?" Bertie asked.

"Up the vent to the roof, with tiles, gutters, chimney and some dozy birds, or down the smelly soil stack to the sewer pipe, up through a drain cover and out into the garden – lots of nightlife, flowers, bushes, trees, a pond and, behind the garden fence, the Tanglewood. The journey pongs, but there's so much more to see."

"Down!" "Up!" was the simultaneous reply, with Bertie

opting for the whiffy, but potentially exciting trip to the garden, while Belinda, ever cautious, preferred the fresher air and the less adventurous upward climb to the roof.

"We'll decide when we get to the junction," Cedric interjected, just in time to prevent another argument. "It will help you to make up your minds."

He led them just a little way along the drain to a spacious opening, where the horizontal tunnel ended, and a wide vertical pipe opened up in front of them. They both walked warily up to the edge, knelt down and peered into the dark precipice. They could SEE nothing, but they were almost knocked back by the smell. They immediately stood up and turned away in a quest for fresh air. After a brief period of recovery, they ventured back to the junction and peeped upwards. An enticing trace of clean air greeted them, and Bertie had made up his mind.

"Perhaps we'll leave the garden till tomorrow, after we've become more acquainted with the atmosphere in the plumbing. I'm sure it'll be interesting up on the roof."

Belinda smiled to herself at Bertie's sudden change of heart but began to consider how they could manage such a long vertical climb.

"I'm not sure we can clamber up that far, Cedric. The drain is too wide for us to push along the sides."

"Not a problem!" retorted the little spider. "You can go up the ladder!"

"Ladder?" Both brushes stared at him in surprise.

"Yes! I guessed you might find it difficult, so I spun a web ladder for you this morning. Do you want to give it a go?"

"Yes please!" they both cried and waited for Cedric to lead the way.

"I'll be on the far side of the vent shaft, so stay level with me. Be careful on the ladder and leave a bit of a gap between you both. Always keep your hands on the side strands and watch where you put your feet – you have smelt what it would be like if you were to slip off! There's a full moon tonight, so it should grow lighter as we ascend. Steady as you go!"

Cedric showed them the ladder, whereupon they reached out to grasp the web and started to climb, with Bertie leading the way. Cedric maintained position on the opposite wall. It wasn't long before they reached the top of the shaft which was open to the air but capped above to prevent the rain coming in. Several of the apertures contained webs which Cedric had spun to catch flies. They looked out to a starry sky and a shiny full moon, enabling them to see clearly the tiled roof and the night garden below.

"The advantage of bright nights like this," Cedric commented, "is that we have very good visibility of everything around us. The disadvantage, on the other hand, is that every creature, friend or enemy, can also see us. However, you, being simple toothbrushes, are in no danger, but I'll have to keep a look out for one or two birds that have a taste for insects, especially juicy spiders like me!"

"We'll look after you, Cedric." Belinda reassured their new companion and Bertie nodded his support. It was at times like this, Cedric reflected, that it was indeed a jolly good thing to have friends.

The three chums made their way out on to the roof and, breathing in the cool night air, they marvelled at the beauty of the night sky which they had only ever seen through the glass of the bathroom window. But as they climbed up the tiles towards the chimney, they heard the harsh trill of a small number of starlings which had made their nest under a loose ridge tile. Just at that moment, a large male bird, with a glossy speckled sheen, poked his head out of the nest and immediately caught sight of Cedric and his two new comrades.

"Well I never!" squawked the starling. "What have we here? I think supper must have arrived! He scuttled down the roof with a very hungry look in his beady eye and went straight for Cedric with beak wide open. The next thing he knew was that his mouth was filled with toothbrush bristles. Bertie had dived straight in, head first, and Belinda had leapt on his back and was shouting "Oh! No! You don't! He's our friend Cedric."

"Your breath smells!" exclaimed Bertie in muffled tones. "You should clean your teeth more often!", without really knowing whether starlings actually had teeth.

"If you leave Cedric alone," said Belinda, "we'll release you and give you and your friends a thorough beak brush. You'll be the smartest starlings on the roof. Now, wag your tail if you agree."

The starling didn't hesitate and shook his tail vigorously, at which Bertie extracted himself from its beak and stood next to Belinda who had jumped back down on to the tiles.

Both of them stood in front of Cedric like royal guards, just in case the starling happened to change his mind.

"Do you have a name?" Belinda enquired, simultaneously introducing herself, Bertie and Cedric.

The starling, still looking rather abashed and flustered after his ordeal, spluttered "Yes. It's S-S-Sturnie," then adding "Errrrr .. I'm s-s-s-sorry, C-C-Cedric. I w-w-won't do it again."

"Never mind, Sturnie," Cedric was more than ready to forgive and forget. "Why don't we do as Belinda suggested and go and visit your family? We can't stay here all night!"

"Oh! .... Yes! Come with me."

Sturnie led them up to the ridge where, under a loose tile, could be heard the chatter of a number of fledgling starling chicks, all of whom had their hungry beaks wide open in anticipation of a night time meal brought back to them by their father.

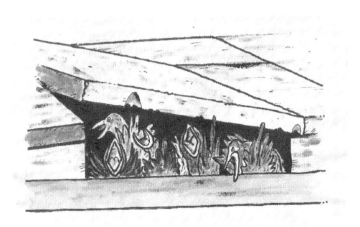

They peered into the nest at the chicks, who looked

both disappointed to see that their father had nothing in his beak with which to satisfy their appetites, and surprised to see three strangers accompanying him, one of whom would appear to have made a very tasty meal.

"Oh," sighed Sturnie glumly, muttering to himself. "How am I going to explain to them that they're not going to eat tonight? It's so difficult being a one parent family."

But Bertie's ears had pricked up. "Blimey! You're not looking after this lot on your own?" he exclaimed bluntly. "Where's their mum?"

"Don't be rude, Bertie! It's none of your business. Please excuse him, Sturnie." Belinda glared at Bertie.

"No. It's O.K. Belinda. Bertie is only saying what you were all thinking. Sadly, I lost my dear Stella to a local sparrowhawk not long ago when she was bringing some worms back for the kids. It swooped down and took her off before I could alert the flock. We can normally defend ourselves well in large numbers and we're magnificent when flying in a murmuration. I find myself having to do the work of two parents these days and feeding the youngsters is particularly demanding."

Cedric interrupted. "Well, we'll soon do something about that. And, in case you're wondering, no, I'm not offering myself as tonight's supper! Wait here, all of you.

Belinda, Bertie, start brushing those hungry beaks. We'll make Sturnie's family the envy of the flock."

Cedric sidled off down the roof, climbed up the air vent, disappeared through an aperture and made his way back to his larder. He emerged a few minutes later dragging a large bundle of dead insects wrapped in a web cocoon. Sturnie flew down to help him and there was a relaxed understanding between them as they tugged the bundle up to the nest, a food parcel for hungry young fledglings. Soon the youngsters were feeding avidly, while Bertie and Belinda were busy grooming their feathers. Even Sturnie had a quick brush up and felt all the better for it.

Cedric, meanwhile, had gone off again to the edge of the nest and was busy spinning webs across every aperture except the main entrance. He then nipped up to the chimney stack and spun some more web traps between the chimney pots.

"These webs should help with your food supply," shouted Cedric from the doorway. "You'll have insects galore soon! Just let me know when the webs are damaged, and I'll pop up to see you and do any necessary repairs. And please tell your friends that I'm most definitely not available for supper and that any insects caught in the chimney webs are at their disposal."

They stayed talking to the youngsters for some time, while Sturnie popped out to tell his neighbours the good news. Word soon spread amongst the starling flock, and, when Belinda, Bertie and Cedric finally said goodbye to Sturnie and his little ones, making their way out of the nest they were escorted back up to the air vent by dozens of cheering starlings. Only time prevented them from accepting offers for a night flight around the neighbourhood.

"Another time, perhaps," Belinda said, thanking the starlings for their kind offer.

"Another adventure." Bertie thought to himself.

"Come on, you two!" called Cedric, "You'll be late home."

Feeling very pleased and excited, the merry trio finally said goodbye to their new friends and made their way back to Cedric's house.

It wasn't long before the toothbrushes had said goodbye to Cedric too, and were moving through the pipes back to the bath plug hole and finally up to their toothbrush rack. They had had a very busy night and settled down quickly and quietly to their usual daily routine.

The following morning, Mr Evershed gave Millie and Bobby their customary morning call. Millie was first to the bathroom, showered, and at the sink to clean her teeth. Picking up Belinda from the rack she noticed a small black speckled feather stuck in the bristles of her brush.

"That's pretty," Millie thought, "but how on earth did it get there?"

Outside the bathroom window, the air was fresh and pleasant, but the morning's silence was suddenly interrupted by a small flock of very noisy, jabbering starlings, who sounded to Millie as though they were attempting to answer her question.

WEDNESDAY NIGHT - THE LILY RAFT

"I've had an exceedingly good idea!" whispered Cedric the Spider, tapping Bertie and Belinda gently on the bristles as they rested in their toothbrush rack. "Come on you two, and don't wake the household!"

"What are you doing here, Cedric? I thought we were going to meet you down the drain." yawned Belinda, but was careful not to disturb the adult toothbrushes, while Bertie, after a big stretch, slipped quietly out of the rack and joined Cedric on the shelf. Belinda immediately followed her younger brother and, moving well away from the rack, she asked again:

"What are we doing, Cedric?"

"Look, do you two want to go out into the garden?"

"Yes!" they both replied eagerly.

"And to go out through the smelly sewage stack?

"Er ... no!" They both shook their heads in unison.

"And all the doors to the outside are shut?"

"Yes," and Belinda added "Mr Evershed always locks up before going to bed. We usually hear him."

"What about the cat flap?"

"Cedric! That's brilliant!" shouted Bertie.

"Shhh!" the other two whispered.

"But how do you know about the cat flap?" Bertie enquired, this time turning the volume down.

"Well, if you'll pardon the pun, I've had a few minor *brushes* outside with Bobby and Millie's cat Florence, but she's far too old and too fat to bother me now. She's asleep on Millie's bed most of the day. No, it's the monster next door we must look out for! His name is Brian. He's a ginger Tom and he's only got three legs – he had an argument with a sports car – but that doesn't prevent him from moving like lightning when he wants to, and he's not averse to playing with spiders if he can't find a bird or a mouse to torment. Come to that, he'd probably toss you two about for fun, even though he couldn't eat you. And in answer to your question, I've watched them both using the cat flap."

"Both?" said Bertie, "but that's our cat Florence's door!"

"Well, Brian doesn't understand ownership. If there's cat food left out on the kitchen floor, he comes in and helps himself. It doesn't happen often, though; Brian has learnt that Florence has usually scoffed the lot by the time he gets there! But we're wasting time. Let's go down the stairs very quietly. Florence may be old, but she's not deaf!"

Bertie, Belinda and Cedric left the bathroom, crossed the landing and descended the staircase. Cedric actually found it easier to slide down the bannister, while the toothbrushes hopped from step to step. Through the kitchen they went, up to the back door and then paused, looking up at the cat flap. Without a word, Bertie leapt up and clung to the base, then heaved himself up in front of the swinging door. He then held out a hand to Belinda, pulling her up to join him. Cedric just walked straight up the door. "How does he do that?" Belinda wondered.

"Now we don't want the flap to rattle and wake all the cats in the neighbourhood," counselled Bertie, who for the moment had taken up the mantle of leadership. "I'll lift the door carefully and hold it open while you two scuttle through. O.K.? Righty-ho, away we go!"

Bertie's plan worked well and, before they knew it, they were all standing outside the back door of the house, gazing down the garden.

"Goodness me," uttered Belinda. "What a fantastic scene, like a magical fairy land. But where do we go from here, Cedric?"

"We'll start by walking down the garden path to the pond. There's always something happening there. But keep your eyes open; you never know what lies around the next corner …!"

The merry trio set off down the garden path, with Belinda and Bertie marvelling at the many sights to behold, even in the moon's half-light: beautiful rose bushes, the lush green lawn, the silhouetted fruit trees and eventually, a glistening expanse of water bounded by reeds, rushes and iridescent purple irises. They had arrived at the garden pond.

"Look, Belinda!" cried Bertie. "I can see the moon swimming in the pond!"

"That's a reflection, stupid," then, thinking she may have been a little harsh, she added "It's like the mirror in the bathroom. It bounces pictures back at you."

Bertie put his nose even closer to the surface of the water and, as he did so, a small wide-eyed face emerged and stared back at him.

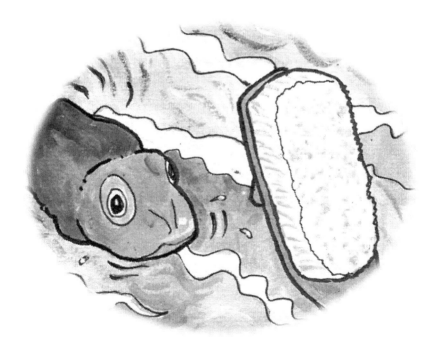

"Who are you staring at?" the creature squeaked, then, gazing intently at Bertie's bristles, continued "Are you a hedgehog? If you are, you're not only very skinny, but you are also the wrong colour. Hedgehogs are certainly not orange. Therefore, I deduce that you are not a hedgehog, just as I am most definitely NOT a common newt. I am not common. I do not even live on a common. That would be most commonplace if I did. I am a SMOOTH newt," she stated, elongating the word 'smooth'. "Only common people call me a common newt. You're not common, are you?"

Bertie, quite taken aback by this babbling outburst, muttered "C-c-common? Er … no, I don't think so. I'm just an ordinary, soft bristle, hygienic, manual toothbrush, like my sister Belinda here. At least, that's what it said on our plastic packaging when we were first purchased by the Eversheds from the chemist shop. My name is Bertie, and our spider friend here is called Cedric."

"Hello Cedric!" said the newt, smoothly.

"Hello Nigella!" replied Cedric.

"Do you two know each other?" enquired Belinda.

"Nigella Newt and I are old friends," explained Cedric, "although she did try to eat me once!"

"What?!" exclaimed the young toothbrushes in disbelief.

"Well, let me explain," Cedric resumed. "I was happily moon-bathing on top of a lily raft over there," he pointed towards a cluster of lily pads on the edge of the pond, "when Nigella, in eager pursuit of a tasty meal, scurried across an adjacent leaf towards me, licking her lips and splashing her tail in the water, when, suddenly, a very large Koi carp caught sight of her wriggling rear end and the hunter became the hunted! 'Watch out!' I yelled, and Nigella pulled her tail quickly from the pond, just in time to see the carp bite a large chunk out of the lily pad that she had been walking on. The carp swam away disappointed, but Nigella uttered a huge sigh of relief and then thanked me profusely."

Nigella took up the story. "Yes. I was so grateful to Cedric. I learnt that I must never again be off my guard when large fish are nearby, and also that help can come from the most unexpected source, even a common spider. Though, of course, you're not common, Cedric," she hastened to point out. "We have been very good friends ever since and he has often helped me to look for the very best raft leaves under which to lay my eggs. He's much better at it than Nigel, my husband, who seems to spend all his time rushing about on land looking for log piles and compost heaps where he can spend the winter."

By now, Nigella had made her way up the pond bank to join the three adventurers and was introduced to Bertie and Belinda by her old friend Cedric.

"How would you fancy a ride on a lily raft?" she asked, "I can paddle you across the pond."

Bertie didn't need asking twice, of course, but Belinda, ever more cautious, asked Nigella if she thought it was safe. "Yes. You'll be fine," she replied, "but stay in the middle of the lily pad and keep a watch out for big fish."

With that, she slid back into the pond and found a lily pad which had been detached from its stem. Then, holding on to it with her four toed, front feet, she used her rear legs and tail to propel it through the water to the bank, where Belinda, Bertie and Cedric hopped on board. They were quick to settle down and, before long were gliding serenely across the water's surface with Nigella providing the paddle which eased them gently forward. Belinda was taking in the all the sights on the pond's rim, the reeds, lilies and water plants as well as a nosey moorhen and her even nosier chicks, who had swum across to see the raft and its occupants. In the meantime, Bertie was leaning precariously over the side watching several busy creatures going about their night time activities: water boatmen, snails, small fishes and a myriad of tadpoles.

A few feet away Ferdinand Frog, discreetly camouflaged, was perched on a large stone on the pond's edge peacefully observing the nightly goings on. He was particularly fascinated by a small group of strange looking creatures floating across the water on a lily pad raft and was about to introduce himself when, out of the corner of his eye, he saw a large, ginger, three-legged, sharp-clawed cat bounding towards him at great speed. Immediately, and instinctively, Ferdinand, who was usually known as Ferdy, hopped as far and as fast as he could out into the pond - SPLASH!!! - just as Brian skidded to a halt on the bank where Ferdy had been sitting. Brian, like most cats, didn't like water and had no intention of pursuing his prey any further. He turned away, snarling with disappointed rage, then set off to look for some tasty mice and rats over by the garden shed.

Unfortunately, in his haste, Ferdy had entered the pond right next to the floating voyagers, causing a tidal wave which upturned the raft and tipped its occupants overboard and into the drink, a dramatic and untimely end to their pleasant moonlight cruise.

Although the water was, by now, quite agitated, Cedric's feather-like body floated easily on the surface and he quickly made his way back to the lily pad.

In the confusion Belinda and Bertie, both being quite used to water from their daily tooth cleaning routines, didn't panic, but looked around for some assistance. Simultaneously, Ferdy and Nigella called "Over here!". Belinda, being a little larger than Bertie, scrambled on to Ferdy's back, while Bertie clung on to Nigella who had straightaway come to his rescue.

With the toothbrushes hitching a ride, Nigella and Ferdy manoeuvred the raft back to the shallow pebble shore where they all made their landing and sat down to rest and get their breath back.

After a breath period of recovery, they all looked at each other and then, as one, burst into laughter.

"That was great!" cried Bertie, "A ride on a raft and on a frog in the same adventure." Then, not forgetting his manners, he thanked Nigella and Ferdy for their help. Cedric, who knew Ferdy from his various excursions to the pond, introduced the toothbrushes formally, but reminded them that they should be getting back to the bathroom soon.

"I must be going, too," squeaked Nigella. "I have some more eggs to lay.

"And me!" croaked Ferdy. "I must keep an eye on my tadpoles. The fish are rather too fond of eating them for breakfast!"

Cedric and the toothbrushes made their way back up the garden path and soon found themselves at the back door looking up at the cat flap.

"Cat! Hide!" shouted Cedric suddenly, and led Bertie and Belinda rapidly across to a hiding place behind a nearby flower pot, just as the cat flap rattled and Florence's head appeared. After the usual wriggle and squeeze, she just about managed to climb through the aperture and waddle down the garden to perform her morning ablutions, without noticing the giggling figures behind the flower pot.

"That was close!" Belinda sighed, "I'm glad it wasn't Brian."

With that, the three of them finally made their way up to the bathroom and said their farewells.

"Will we see you tomorrow night?" asked Bertie, as Cedric scuttled off towards the bath. The little spider half turned and grinned, waving one of his many legs vaguely in their direction.

The small toothbrushes climbed up to their rack and were just about to jump into their slots, when one of the adult brushes, who had been watching them, leant across and whispered in their ears, "Get in quickly and don't disturb Mrs Brush. We'll speak about your night time activities in the morning when the humans have left the house."

At around 8 o'clock the following morning, Bobby Evershed was about to clean his teeth when he noticed a small black tadpole in the bristles of his orange toothbrush. Fortunately, he was neither a curious nor a fussy boy and simply flushed the creature down the sink and started brushing.

Terence, the Tadpole, spent the rest of the day swimming in the water trap in the U bend under the sink, but Bertie, suddenly realising what had happened, knew that for Ferdy's sake he had to rescue the little creature at the first opportunity.

THURSDAY NIGHT - DOCTOR GOBLINS

It was 9 o'clock on Thursday morning. The house was empty; Mr and Mrs Evershed had both gone to work, while Millie and Bobby were sitting in their respective classes at the local primary school. At the same time, up in the bathroom at number 24, March Meadow, Belinda and Bertie were resting in their toothbrush rack after last night's exhausting escapade at the garden pond. They were, however, woken by a firm adult voice coming from behind them.

The brush which they had always known as their father spoke quietly, but with a serious tone.

"Pay attention, you two. I have to explain a thing or two about toothbrushes," he began. "You see, toothbrushes are not like human beings. They are just things! They cannot walk or talk or have baby toothbrushes and they have no life in them. They are just made of plastic in a factory and are simply there to clean human teeth, which, by the way, happens to be a very good thing. When their bristles wear out, the humans simply throw them away, or use them to clean small, hard-to-reach areas, such as the edges of taps and tiles. All four of us were bought from the local chemist, you two just a week or so after your mother and me, and we were no different at that time from any other toothbrush. So, strictly speaking, we are not actually your parents."

This came as quite a shock to the young toothbrushes. "But we can all walk and talk," protested Belinda, with Bertie nodding in agreement. "Why are we different? Bertie and I have always known you as our mum and dad."

"And you shall continue to do so," said their mother, reassuringly.

Mr Brush continued. "Not long after you two were put next to your mother and me in the rack, a very strange thing happened, though, of course, we didn't learn the full details of it until afterwards. It was night time on a very hot June evening and the bathroom window was wide open to let in some fresh air. Outside, behind the garden fence, and deep in Tanglewood, it so happened that two doctor goblins were having a heated argument."

"Doctor goblins???!!!" they both exclaimed. "What on earth are they?"

"Well," their father continued, "goblins are short, rather ugly, bad-tempered woodland creatures who look a bit like humans. They are quite small, about milk bottle height. Their heads are too big for their bodies, their ears are large and pointed and they have nasty, little, beady red eyes."

"I wouldn't like to meet one of those!" Belinda noted.

"However," Mr Brush resumed, emphasising the word 'however', "they are extremely clever, and know all about plants, roots and berries, which they often use to treat illnesses and make animals better. That's why we call them doctor goblins. Humans also use nature's flowers and shrubs in much the same way, but their knowledge is very limited compared to goblins. They also write about goblins in their fairy tales, but they don't believe that they really exist.

Goblins are mysterious creatures who like to keep themselves to themselves, but, despite their rather unpleasant appearance and grumpy disposition, they are mostly, at heart, very kind individuals who hate to see animals suffering. They have a large range of medicine, pills and potions. It is even said that they have, on occasions, actually brought dead animals back to life by a mysterious practice they call 'cobalus' which involves rubbing their pointed ears and staring at the animal!"

"So, what were the two doctor goblins arguing about?" Bertie asked impatiently.

"Exactly that! Ten Ends, the grumpiest goblin in the wood, didn't believe that his rival Locum, the wisest and most knowledgeable goblin of the Tanglewood tribe, could actually use cobalus on something that had died.

Locum argued, modestly, that given the right circumstances and conditions, it might even be possible to generate life in an inanimate or lifeless object like a stone. To settle their dispute, they waited until nightfall, then headed off to the largest oak tree in the wood, which happened to be the stately home of Wye's Owl, the very clever night bird, who was renowned for his knowledge, judgement and wisdom."

Mrs Brush, meanwhile, was smiling at her little family. She had always wanted things to be explained to her children. Belinda and Bertie were listening intently as their father continued.

"When he heard the squabbling goblins approaching, Wye's Owl, who spoke with a gently lilting, Welsh accent, flew down from his nest, and hooted indignantly 'Tu whit, tu whoo! What's the meaning of this disturbance?' The goblins were immediately scared into silence and then, after a short pause, Ten Ends, irritable as ever, gave the reasons for their quarrel and asked the owl to say who was correct, but also happened to mention that Locum was talking nonsense if he thought that he could bring life into a lifeless object by staring and rubbing his ears.

'We'll see about that,' Wye's Owl pondered thoughtfully … 'Let's take a little trip, shall we? Follow me!' He led them away to the edge of the wood, then into the back garden of our house, where Wye's Owl stopped and looked up at the wide-open bathroom window.

'Jump on my back, you two,' he ordered. The goblins were far too fearful of him to disobey and climbed aboard. Wye's was a very large, male tawny owl, at least twice as long as the doctor goblins, and he had no

problem flying the short distance up to the bathroom carrying his two rear passengers. With the owl keeping watch at the window, Locum and Ten Ends climbed through, looked carefully around them and, after some consideration of the size and shape of the items they would choose for their test, made their way across to the toothbrush rack.

Locum stared intently at the largest toothbrush, gently

rubbing his glowing ears ..."

After a brief pause, Mr Brush continued. "Suddenly I became conscious of a tingling sensation in my arms and legs. My eyes opened, I had ears which suddenly could hear things and a mind which could actually think. I then realised that I had become alive, after which I slowly became aware of my body, my size, my shape, my home and my bathroom surroundings! Lastly, I stared at the two strange creatures in front of me and listened as Locum explained in detail everything that had happened to me, what I had been before and what I was now. The sour-faced Ten Ends had, begrudgingly, lost the argument with Locum and was looking very annoyed and resentful. I was now a living toothbrush, and, shortly afterwards, Locum gave the gift of life to your mother as well."

"But what about us?" Bertie asked.

"Your mother and I asked the doctor goblins to leave you as you were for a while until we had learned more about ourselves, our house, the family here and what it was really like to be a living toothbrush. Like you, we did some exploring, both indoors and outdoors, and soon met some of your friends, including Cedric. At that point, we decided that it was safe for you two to join us. Locum came again and used cobalus to bring you both to life a few weeks later, while you were resting, and then we decided to give you some time and space to explore the world for yourselves, without any interference from us."

"You know Cedric?" asked Belinda.

"Yes. Of course, we do. He's a very helpful and kind little spider. Once we had got to know him, we recruited him to keep a quiet eye on you two, and he's done a very good job!"

"He didn't let on," Belinda commented.

"And two more pieces of advice before we leave you alone," said Mr Brush.

"Firstly, you must keep all this to yourselves and respect the secrets of the doctor goblins and the other animals you encounter. You must not put them in danger. Humans know nothing about our little world, even if they think they do. We all want it to stay that way."

"Secondly, you are very fortunate. Unlike other toothbrushes, your handles and bristles will not wear out, so the humans will not need to throw you away. Therefore, you must be very careful not to make them suspect that you are different in other ways, too. You must not leave any more evidence of your night time adventures, like starling feathers, Belinda, and tadpoles, Bertie. We've been watching what you've been up to!"

"Tadpoles!" shrieked Bertie. "I've just remembered. We must rescue the little tadpole which Bobby washed down the sink!"

"Yes. We must." Mr Brush agreed. "But be patient. Bobby was the last person to use the sink this morning."

"And every morning!" piped in Belinda, "He's always the last up."

"Which means," her father carried on, "that the little tadpole is probably still in the U bend water trap under the sink and hasn't been washed away. First, you must get him out before the family uses the sink when they return home this evening, and then somehow, tonight, you must get him back to the pond. Your mother and I will leave you two to sort out that little problem. You can ask us for help if you need it, and you mustn't leave the bathroom before everyone has gone to bed. It's far too dangerous to leave the house in the daylight. You'll be seen."

Mr and Mrs Brush left the youngsters to their thoughts and returned to their own daily routine.

"What can we do?" asked Bertie. Belinda sat pondering for a while on the bathroom shelf before she spoke.

"We must first check that he's still there. Then we must find a cup or something in the house which we can fill with water and where we can leave him safely until tonight. Then we can take him back to the pond. He can obviously survive out of water for a short time."

"How do you know, Belinda?"

"Because he came back to the house in your bristles last night, idiot!"

"Oh yes," said Bertie, finally catching on. "Look, I'll go and check that the tadpole hasn't been washed away and is still O.K. In the meantime, you go and find Cedric. Maybe he'll have some ideas."

Bertie jumped from the shelf into the sink and was soon down the plug hole staring at the water trap.

"Are you there, tadpole?" He called out several times and, eventually, the tiny creature swam to the surface.

"If you can understand me, waggle your tail three times." I hope he can count, Bertie thought to himself.

Sure enough, Terence Tadpole wiggled his tail three times.

"Listen! We're going to find you a safer place to hide. You'll be washed away if you stay here. Then, tonight, we'll take you back to your pond. O.K.? Just wait there a little longer and I'll be back."

Terence wiggled his tail three times and Bertie thought he saw a relieved smile on the small creature's face.

He then returned to the toothbrush rack to find Cedric standing there with Belinda.

"He's there, and he's safe," called Bertie. "We've just got to get him out."

"Tell him your plan, Cedric," Belinda had managed to find the little spider in the air vent and had brought him back to help.

"Right, Bertie. Go and fetch the tadpole now and bring him back here in your bristles."

Bertie rushed off again and brought back the frightened little tadpole who just managed to tell them that his name was Terence and that he was one of Ferdy's boys.

"Well done," said Cedric. "Now come with me; he's out of water so there's no time to lose. I'll explain as we go." They hurried out of the bathroom and down the stairs. The house was quiet except for the sound of Florence Cat snoring in one of the bedrooms. Once in the kitchen, Cedric walked up a cupboard door by the sink on to the shiny marble work surface, simultaneously spinning a ladder web for his companions to climb up and join him, with Terence clinging on to Bertie's bristles. On the kitchen window sill, there was a small flower vase containing some pretty sweet peas of several different colours standing in some fresh water.

"You must go in there, Terence, until late at night, when we'll come and take you back to the pond. But hide among the flower stems and keep out of sight. Be brave, now." Bertie lifted Terence from the back of his head and dropped him into the flower vase. They all waved goodbye to the little tadpole before returning quickly to their homes, Bertie and Belinda up the stairs to the bathroom and Cedric down through the kitchen sink plug hole ...

It was midnight, the humans had all gone to bed and the three friends had met up in the bathroom and crept downstairs to the kitchen. Mrs Evershed, who kept a clean house, had noticed a cobweb on the kitchen cupboard, and cleared it away with her duster, meaning that Cedric had to spin another web ladder. What would Mrs Evershed think when she saw another spider web in the same place the next morning!

They reached the flower vase, and, to their relief, Terence was still inside. Bertie tapped on the glass and indicated for the tadpole to take a deep breath before he lifted him out. He then popped Terence up into his bristles and hastily joined the others as they scrambled down the ladder and across to the cat flap. In their haste, they caused the flap to rattle more than usual, a noise which attracted the unwanted attention of Brian, the three-legged ginger tom from next door. The rescue party hid behind the nearest flower pot until Brian had lost interest and skulked off. However, precious time had been lost and Terence was beginning to suffer.

By the time they had reached the pond and found Ferdy Frog it became very clear to all of them that Terence wasn't going to make it. They lowered him into the water, but it had no effect. The little tadpole floated still and lifeless on the surface. Bertie and Belinda were in tears. All their efforts had been in vain and they felt helpless and hopeless.

At this moment, Cedric disappeared without saying a word, leaving the toothbrushes and Ferdy anxious and distraught. Bertie, who blamed himself for Terence's death, spoke first "We told Terence to be brave; we must be brave too. I'm sure Cedric hasn't deserted us. He's such a decent spider."

Nigella arrived and tried to console them and spent a few moments with Ferdy alone. Life was difficult and dangerous for young newts and tadpoles.

Just as the young toothbrushes were about to give up and go back to the house to look for Cedric, a familiar voice was heard behind them. They turned to see Cedric himself, accompanied by a small weird looking creature, which they immediately recognised from their father's description as a doctor goblin.

"Where is the patient?" he snapped abruptly, and, ignoring the toothbrushes, he was shown to the pond bank by Nigella. Locum bent over, held Terence in the water, squeezed and released his gills several times and blew gently into his face. After what seemed to Bertie and Belinda to be a lifetime, the little tadpole jerked, wriggled his tail and swam off towards his father.

FRIDAY NIGHT - TANGLEWOOD

The doctor goblins, Mr and Mrs Ends, were sitting down in their living room, looking back nostalgically over the 50 years that they had been married. They had had a good life in Tanglewood bringing up a large family of 12 children whom they had named numerically – One Ends, Two Ends, Three Ends etc. The family had been well provided for and had never had to go without. But their one sorrow, amidst all the happy moments and memories, was their tenth child, Ten Ends.

Ten Ends had been a difficult boy from the beginning, spiteful, selfish and disobedient, even though his parents, brothers and sisters had tried their best to help and understand him. He grew up to possess all the nasty qualities which you might associate with goblins, but with none of their redeeming features such as kindness and a desire to help others, especially the sick.

Then, as he grew more withdrawn and reclusive, he began to lose the very quality that characterises the Tanglewood goblins, the gift of healing.

Locum, on the other hand, discovered that the more he helped other animals with his kind nature and healing powers, the more those powers grew. Birds with broken wings, squirrels with tooth infections, bats which had faulty radar, all came to see Locum for treatment, while Ten Ends became more jealous and resentful. He began to hate Locum, even more so since the argument over 'cobalus' when he had brought the toothbrushes to life.

On Friday night, at home in March Meadow, with the Evershed family comfortably asleep in bed, Bertie and Belinda had travelled through the bath pipework and were chatting to their friend Cedric the Spider in his cosy air vent home.

"Where shall we go tonight, Cedric?" asked Bertie, eager to get on the move and enjoy another adventure with Cedric and his sister.

Before Cedric could answer, Belinda made a suggestion: "I'd like to visit Tanglewood to say thank you to Locum for healing Terence Tadpole. It was so awful when we thought that we'd lost him, and I'll never forget Ferdy's face when Terence recovered and swam towards him. We were all so relieved!"

Cedric pondered. "Tanglewood has its dangers, you know, although I understand why you want to go there. Nevertheless, we'll have to be even more careful than usual. Now how shall we travel? By land or by air?"

"What do you mean, 'by air'?" the young toothbrushes queried.

"Well," Cedric continued, "Sturnie Starling and his friends owe me a favour. I've been spinning and repairing web traps to help them catch insects for their meals. I could ask them to fly us out to the large oak tree in Tanglewood where Wye's Owl lives. Wye's will help us to get in touch with the goblins."

Bertie and Belinda both considered that this was the quickest, safest and easily the most exciting option. They wouldn't have to creep through the house, cat flap and garden risking an unpleasant encounter with the local cat and rat populations, and they'd both be able to enjoy a flight on 'Starling Airlines'. In a moment the three of them were journeying up the air vent to the roof.

Sturnie's chicks had undoubtedly grown since Bertie and Belinda had last seen them. The fly traps had done their job and the fledglings were no longer short of food. Their wing feathers were developing, and they would soon be leaving the nest and taking to the air. They all seemed very pleased to see their visitors and Cedric in particular, whom they regarded as their friend and benefactor, and thought of as one of their family.

Sturnie was keen to help Cedric and his two friends and agreed to transport them to Tanglewood. While he flew off to enlist some help, Belinda and Bertie gave the chicks a quick grooming and they warbled with delight as the toothbrushes stroked softly through their feathery down. It wasn't long before Sturnie returned with the couple next door, Sid and Shirley, who had also enjoyed the fruits of Cedric's chimney web traps and said that they felt honoured to give their new friends an air lift to the great oak, the woodland home of Wye's Owl.

Belinda really took to Shirley, who chattered merrily away about her young fledglings, how cheeky they were, how they were constantly hungry, and it wasn't long before the two of them had become good friends. Bertie wanted Sid to tell him everything about flying, how difficult it was, whether he could fly, and how Sid navigated when he was in the air.

"Flying comes naturally to us," began Sid. "We have very light bodies and powerful wings. We find our way just as you do on the ground, looking out for recognisable landmarks like the church tower, the Town Hall clock , and the familiar features of our little cul-de-sac in March Meadow. We love to fly out to the telephone wires on the edge of Tanglewood, where we often gather in large numbers to chat about the weather conditions and the gossip of the day."

In the meantime, Cedric had discussed the flight details with Sturnie and had crawled up on to his back, simultaneously calling the others to prepare for take-off. Bertie eagerly jumped up on to Sid, whilst Shirley instructed Belinda to hop on board. With a thrust of their muscular wings, the three starlings were instantly in the air and setting a circular course for Tanglewood. The purpose of avoiding the direct route was to survey a wider area and check for potential risks and hazards, but this, of course, didn't bother Bertie, who was having a wonderful time soaring through the air with the wind rushing through his bristles.

Before long, they were flying over Tanglewood towards a massive oak tree, at least 100 feet tall, towering above the other trees in the surrounding canopy like a king on a pedestal overlooking his subjects.

"Here we go!" Sturnie called back to the others in his small aerial formation. "Prepare to land!" The three birds and their passengers flew through the tree tops and down to a huge branch about half way up the oak, and just below the crowns of the neighbouring trees, thereby making them invisible to any birds of prey flying above the wood. Just above their landing place, in a cavity in the main trunk where a branch had once broken away, sat a very large tawny owl looking down at them with huge, round, binocular eyes.

"I was beginning tu whit to wonder when I might meet you two characters," Wye's Owl tooted in soft, though considered Welsh tones, as he looked Belinda and Bertie up and down. "I've heard all about you, of course, you're quite the talk of the wood, and I was present when

Locum awakened the spirit in your toothbrush parents. Now what brings you to my humble home?"

"Hardly humble," Belinda thought to herself. "It's enormous …."

At this point, the starlings, always in awe of this formidable and legendary bird, quietly flew off back to their nests, with Shirley muttering something about getting back to feed the chicks.

Belinda looked up at Wye's Owl and explained. "Well, your honour …" at which point the mighty bird immediately interrupted: "I'm not 'Your Honour'. I'm not a High Court Judge, I'm just an owl. If you must address me formally, 'Mr Tawny' will do nicely."

Belinda began again: "We're very sorry to disturb you, Mr Tawny, but we wish to find Locum, the doctor goblin. He saved our friend Terence's life yesterday and we blame ourselves for Terence being out of the pond. We just want to thank Locum properly."

Belinda went on to describe the events of the last two nights, although she had the distinct feeling that the owl already knew everything that had happened. This reminded her of an ancient nursery rhyme she had once heard Millie's mother reading to her daughter:

The wise old owl lived in the oak. The more he heard, the less he spoke;

The less he spoke, the more he heard. Wasn't he a wise old bird?!

"Mmmm ... yes ... mmmm ... the young tadpole ... Ferdy's boy," Mr Tawny muttered. "I happened tu whit to hear all about that. Let me see now ..." he paused again before continuing, "In normal circumstances, I'd advise you to stay well away from the goblins; they can be quite unpleasant at times. But as it's my good friend Locum, and he's a worthy fellow, I'll point you in the right direction. Don't leave the path I show you and keep a sharp eye out for anything unusual. Let Cedric do the talking if anything approaches you. Remember, you will not be recognised as a woodland creature, and even good-natured animals will be wary of you; and if you do find yourselves in difficulty, just shout 'Specky'. Cedric will understand."

"Specky?" both brushes looked puzzled but noticed that Cedric was discreetly shaking his head at them to deter any further questions. Instead, they listened carefully to Mr Tawny's closing instructions ...

For the second time that night, the intrepid trio were in flight, this time on Wye's Owl's back flying down to the floor of the wood, which, to the three diminutive friends, seemed more like a vast forest. Faint glimmers of moonlight shone in patches through the tree tops, but they could just make out a narrow, winding path, edged by brambles, saplings and spreading ferns, leading away from them into the dark depths of the wood.

"Follow this path to the stream," Wye's Owl directed them, "then cross over – it's quite shallow – and take the left fork at the silver birch tree. By then, Locum will know you are coming and will come to meet you." With that, he flew suddenly and silently back up to his nest.

Where Wye's Owl, Cedric and the doctor goblins were concerned, the young toothbrushes had learnt by now not to ask silly questions like 'How will he know we're coming?' These creatures all seemed to have a sixth sense as to the goings on in the natural world about them and the local bush telegraph seemed to work most effectively. So, as they set off down the path, Belinda and Bertie were not surprised that many curious eyes were watching their progress, both from above and below, with others peering out at them from the shadowy undergrowth. Their feelings fluctuated between fear and excitement, uneasiness and expectation, just as the woodland backdrop flickered between light and darkness. In particular, Belinda felt the presence of a tiny, living, twinkling star frequently orbiting around them.

They eventually reached the stream which they crossed with Cedric sitting on Belinda's head, and finally arrived at the silver birch where the path divided.

"Which way did Mr Tawny say?" Bertie asked, to which both Cedric and Belinda immediately retorted "Left!"

They followed the left-hand path for some time until, out of the darkness ahead, the shadowy outline of a small goblin appeared.

"Is that you, Doctor Locum?" Belinda called, giving Locum the title to which she thought he was entitled.

There was a sinister and lengthy silence.

"Locum?" she repeated. Another pause, then ...

"I've been waiting for you three."

The voice was sneering and full of malice. Emerging into the half-light, a short, loathsome, repulsive goblin appeared and made his way threateningly towards them.

"Welcome to Tanglewood Deep!" the goblin squealed, in a voice which was anything but welcoming.

"Who are you?" enquired Belinda. "Where's Locum? He was supposed to meet us here."

Cedric said nothing at this point, although he instantly recognised the creature addressing them. It was Ten Ends, a nasty, ill-natured, jealous goblin who was known to dislike Locum intensely. The little spider suspected some sort of trap but hoped that he had flown under Ten Ends' radar in the past and thought that it might be useful to play the innocent for the time being, while remaining on high alert.

"Locum was feeling a little under the weather today, probably a chill or a bug he picked up from his exploits in the pond last night. Stupid fellow, risking his own health for a worthless tadpole. As if there aren't enough of them already."

Bertie and Belinda were both about to dispute this point, but noticed Cedric again shaking his head gently at them. This was not the time for an argument. They had to find Locum.

Cedric spoke up. "Can you please direct us to Locum's house? The toothbrushes here wish to speak to him."

"It would be my pleasure," the goblin replied obsequiously, "although he's resting at my place today. Come with me, and I'll take you there."

They followed Ten Ends further into Tanglewood Deep, appropriately named, as the undergrowth and the silence became denser still. No longer were there any watching eyes; even the bravest birds and animals didn't venture here.

They eventually arrived at a small, fern-covered hump in the ground, at the back of which was a narrow, half-hidden passage which led inside. Ten Ends lit a single candle and, as their eyes became accustomed to the dim light, the three friends looked around them at the gloomy room which was the goblin's home; a dirty rug, a table, a rocking chair, a small chest of drawers, and a food larder. Locum was nowhere to be seen.

"I expect you wish to know the whereabouts of your friend Locum. Well, be patient. Oh, I've forgotten my manners. Can I get you something to drink? I have prepared a very refreshing 'fruits of the forest' cordial."

They looked at each other hesitantly before politely saying no.

"As you please." Ten Ends continued disdainfully, "Then you'd better come with me ..."

He led them to a door at the back of the room which he unlocked before ushering them inside. There, on a small hay bed, with his feet and hands bound tight with twine, lay Locum, semi-conscious and with a sickly grey pallor. The three companions were horrified and rushed across to help him. At that moment they heard the door shut behind them and the key turn in the lock. They were in complete darkness and were trapped inside.

"Stand back!" instructed Cedric, "Let me look at him. We spiders don't need our eyes. We use touch, taste and vibration to see. Now try to find a candle or sky light and loosen those bonds on his hands and feet."

As the spider tended to Locum, the goblin slowly and

feebly explained the train of events which had allowed Ten Ends to get the better of him. "He met me as I was returning from the pond last night and congratulated me for resuscitating poor Terence. How stupid I was. Misplaced pride in what I had done made me drop my guard. I should have realised that he was up to something. He suggested that we toasted my success with a drink and poured me one of his fruit cordials. That was all I can remember till I woke up here. I suspect that he'd laced my drink with valerian root - it can have a knockout punch – then dragged me over to his house."

"Now we know why he offered us a drink," said Bertie.

"And why he looked so disappointed when we refused it." added Belinda.

By now they had both succeeded in releasing Locum's hands and feet.

"I think he intended to use me as a bait to get at you toothbrushes. He hated it when I brought you and your parents into the living world. I think he might try to turn you all back to lifeless plastic. It's much easier to take life away than to give it. He has some very nasty potions."

"We must get out of here," Belinda cried despairingly. "What can we do? I can't see a thing."

"Call Specky!" Cedric blurted out suddenly, "We must call Specky. Just do it!!"

The toothbrushes shouted as loud as they could: "SPECKY!!!"

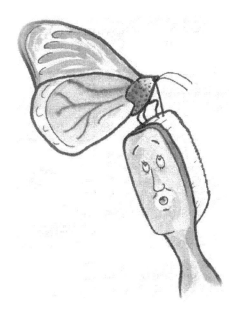

"No one will hear us down here." Bertie looked despondent.

Just then, a small speckled butterfly landed on Belinda's bristles. Belinda immediately put two and two together.

"It was you, wasn't it? You were that flickering light. You've been following us all the time."

Specky, a small speckled wood butterfly, introduced herself briefly in a sweet, lisping voice. Like the Brush family, she also had been given extended life by Locum, who, in turn, used her knowledge to make medicine from the pollen she collected. She also had another job – as Wye's Owl's secret spy.

"Ask him for a drink," she said. "He'll be delighted to provide one for you! Just don't drink it. When he opens the door, I'll slip away unseen and go to fetch help. Mr Tawny will have something to say about this little episode."

"Actually," croaked Locum weakly, "You two can drink it. It will have no effect on your plastic tummies, but I don't suppose that he realises that."

"Even better," twittered Specky. "Now; call him. We have little time to lose."

Bertie, who had the loudest voice, shouted out "Can we please have a drink; it's very dry and dusty in here."

A sarcastic, mocking voice replied. "So, you've decided to be polite and accept my hospitality, have you? Wait there. Oh, I forgot! You haven't any choice, have you!!!"

A moment or two later he was at the door. "No tricks, mind you. I have my scalpel here. Stand back!"

The prisoners moved to the back of the room as the

door was unlocked and opened. Ten Ends didn't notice a tiny flicker of light flashing past his head as he brought in a tray of drinks which he carried in one hand, but with a sharp surgeon's scalpel in the other. He passed the drinks round to everyone except Locum, who was still lying half-asleep on the floor, then picking up the goblet which he had carefully reserved for himself, raised it high, and said aloud, "Your health," though he failed to say whether that might be good or bad. Pouring the harmless cordial down his throat, he then watched carefully as Bertie and Belinda drank the toxic cocktail that they had been given. But his obsessive hatred of the toothbrushes meant that he momentarily took his eye off Cedric, who quickly tipped the contents of his tiny cup into a goblin shoe on the floor.

Bertie and Belinda performed their acting role brilliantly, suddenly gripping their throats, rolling their eyes, spluttering, staring at each other and moaning agonisingly, before falling to the floor, seemingly lifeless. Cedric had used the opportunity to slide quietly up the wall above the bed and was hiding behind a strip of wood on the ceiling. Meanwhile Ten Ends forced some more sleeping potion into Locum and refastened his twine bonds. He then lifted Bertie and Belinda into a small wooden chest by his bed and returned to his sitting room, locking the bedroom door behind him. Finally, he sat down in his rocking chair, more than satisfied with his night's work, and nodded off to sleep.

Half an hour or so later, and not long before sunrise, he was rudely awakened by a huge bird crashing through his doorway. Before he could respond, a giant claw had lifted him into the air and he found himself staring into the largest eyes and the sharpest bird beak he had ever seen.

"I should bite you in half," Wye's Owl growled, "But YOU would give me dog breath. Now open that door before I change my mind; and may the Green Man of the Woods help you if any harm has come to my guests!"

Thinking that he had actually silenced the toothbrushes forever, Ten Ends was beside himself with fear. He dreaded to think of the punishment that Wye's Owl would impose on him. He tried to stall ...

"They left a while back, Mr Tawny" he spluttered. "Locum wasn't well, so I was looking after him and told them he mustn't be disturbed. They didn't want to make him worse. They just went away. They are probably lost. I could help you look for them if you like. Please don't hurt me! Please put me down!"

"OPEN THAT DOOR!" the owl boomed menacingly, throwing Ten Ends down to the floor.

Without further delay, Ten Ends did as he was commanded and unlocked the door to reveal the dismal scene. Locum was out cold, and looking groggier than ever, but a small voice called down to Wye's Owl:

"Mr Tawny! They're in the chest!"

"Thank you, Cedric. Now you ..." he barked, glaring at Ten Ends, "Open it!"

Ten Ends had no defiance left in him and meekly did as he was ordered, dreading the consequences of his deeds. His reaction on discovering two grinning toothbrushes staring at him as he lifted the lid, was complete bewilderment. On the one hand, he was hopeful that his punishment might be reduced as they were both still very much alive, while on the other, he felt thwarted that his malicious plan had failed and that the toothbrushes had survived unharmed. He knew, too, that there would be serious consequences for the suffering he had inflicted on Locum.

"I'll deal with you tu whit tomorrow, you despicable creature," Wye's Owl glowered at Ten Ends with a fierce, penetrating stare, "but just now there isn't any time. I must take care of Locum, and," he continued, turning to look at Cedric, Bertie and Belinda, "I must fly you three back home as quickly as possible! The humans will soon be rising."

SATURDAY NIGHT - THE TOOL SHED

Everyone who lived at number 24, March Meadow loved Saturdays, everyone except Bertie Brush.

Millie and Bobby Evershed didn't have to go to school, and their parents were at home most of the day, which meant that the bathroom was in frequent use. In the toothbrush rack, Mr and Mrs Brush and their daughter Belinda enjoyed watching the bustle of activity and listening to all the family gossip, but Bertie couldn't wait for the time when everyone was tucked up in bed and he could set off on another escapade. What made matters worse was that the humans always stayed up later than usual on Saturday night, perhaps watching a film, entertaining friends or enjoying a take-away meal.

"At last!" Bertie exclaimed, "I thought that the Wilsons would never go home." It was well after midnight and the house was at last silent. "Let's hope that they all have a lie in tomorrow morning. Come on, Belinda. Let's go and find Cedric."

"Mind how you go, you two!" The mild words of warning came from Mrs Brush, who didn't care to imagine what 'you two' got up to on their nightly exploits.

Cedric was inspecting his larder when the brushes arrived. By now they were quite familiar with the route from the bath plug hole to Cedric's snug, air vent home and no longer required the use of the guiding thread which Cedric had spun for them.

"The fly supplies are getting a bit low," Cedric commented as he greeted them. "The starlings have been emptying all the rooftop webs, so I'll need to make a trip to the garden shed tonight. I've set up a number of insect traps on the roof under the eaves and gutters. You two can help me carry the foodstuff back, if you don't mind?"

"We'd be pleased to help, Cedric," said Belinda politely. "Come on, Bertie. Let's get going!"

As they left the bathroom, they crept stealthily past Florence, the Evershed's family moggy, who was lying fast asleep on the landing, a very podgy black and white lump of snoring fur.

The brushes giggled all the way down the stairs, despite

Cedric's appeals for silence. Across the kitchen and out through the cat flap, they were soon making their way down the garden path towards the shed.

"Kerraaash! Clunk! From three doors down the road, the metallic clang of a dustbin being upturned rang through the still night air, while its lid rolled away a couple of spins before itself banging on to the concrete paving.

"What on earth was that?" asked the toothbrushes, startled by the sudden commotion.

"Oh, that'll be the night raiders," answered Cedric wearily, "either Boris or Philip, looking for a fast food supper. There's always plenty of that in the bins on Saturday night; chicken bones, fish batter, greasy kebabs, hardly a healthy diet for foxes and badgers, or for humans, too, come to that!"

"Foxes and badgers?!!" Bertie cried.

"This gets worse," Belinda muttered to herself.

"Yes, Boris Badger and Philip Fox, both fat, lazy blighters who can't be bothered to hunt for proper food, so they scavenge the bins. You're bound to bump into them at some time but don't worry, despite their size they're pretty harmless, just rowdy and stupid. Ignore them for now, we've got work to do."

They continued to the bottom of the garden and past the compost heap, where the path turned a corner and led across the lawn to Mr Evershed's old brown tool shed. As they approached, two dashing figures shot across the grass in front of them, one in hot pursuit of the other, causing Bertie, Belinda and Cedric to sprint for cover behind a large blackcurrant bush. Brian, the mad ginger, three-legged tom cat from next door, was hurtling after a large brown rat.

Fortunately for her, Roxie Rat reached the shelter of the tool shed just as Brian pounced. She quickly scuttled under the shed base, between the paving slabs on which the supporting timbers rested, and into the rubble and soil foundation, where she stopped to catch her breath.

Brian's final leap was misjudged, with the result that he banged his head on the shed floor, bounced backwards, shook himself down and slunk away disappointedly, too big to squeeze through the rat's escape passageway. Slightly dazed, he pondered on the lack of success he had had that week with high speed chases. Perhaps he was losing his touch.

"We'd better go and see if Roxie is O.K." Cedric whispered, looking round to make sure that Brian was no longer on the scene.

"Roxie?" Both toothbrushes gaped at Cedric in amazement. "You know that rat?"

"Yes, of course," Cedric declared, "she's an old friend. But she shouldn't be rushing around like that in her state."

"Her state?" Belinda's face was a picture of curiosity. "She isn't …"

Cedric butted in. "Yes, she is. More little ratlets due next week. Come along, we'll pay a visit to Rat Manor!"

Without any delay, Cedric scampered across the lawn towards the shed, with Bertie and Belinda trailing behind, both full of misgivings about setting foot inside a rat burrow.

"Hurry up, you two, and mind your heads when you duck down under here."

The two brushes followed Cedric under the tool shed, stooping low to avoid the wooden beams, until they reached the entrance to the rat burrow where they found Roxie Rat, sitting back on her haunches, mopping her brow with her front paws.

"That perishin' cat!" she exclaimed, "Hasn't he better things to do than to chase after an expectant mother …! Oh, hello Cedric. I didn't see you there; what brings you here … and who are your friends?"

Cedric introduced Bertie and Belinda who were delighted to meet such a cheery rat. "We were coming over to check my fly traps when we saw Brian on your tail. We just popped in to see if you're O.K."

"Well, that's very kind of you and I'm fine, thank you, despite Brian's worst intentions. But now you're here, you'd better come inside and say hello to the ratlets. I'm sure they'd all like to meet Bertie and Belinda. Oh!" Roxie had a sudden moment of realisation. "I've just put two and two together. Weren't you all in Tanglewood last night with the doctor goblins? Well! We may have a little surprise for you!"

They followed Roxie into a short tunnel which served as the entrance to Rat Manor. Once their eyes had adjusted to the near darkness, they observed that the burrow itself was the home for a small pack of four rat families, each living in separate nests made from twigs, straw and household debris, such as strips of paper and cardboard. What amazed the young toothbrushes was how clean and tidy everything was. The nests themselves were very neatly constructed and the general floor area was spotless. The young rats were very well groomed with fur that shone in the dark.

But it was when they looked across to the far side of the hollow, that they had the biggest shock of all. There, stooping over meekly, with a small broom in his hands sweeping the floor, stood Ten Ends, the malicious doctor goblin who had been the cause of such appalling distress the night before.

"What on earth is he doing here?" Belinda asked, "I thought we'd seen the last of him."

"He's serving his punishment," explained Roxie, "100 hours Community Service. Wye's Owl brought him here this morning to work in Rat Manor. He has to clean the nests, sweep the floors, and apply flea treatment to the ratlets. Surprisingly, it transpires that he's quite good at it and appears to enjoy looking after my little ones. Let's hope he's started to turn over a new leaf. To help matters, Locum also popped in with flea drops and some other potions which Ten Ends can use."

"But won't he try to escape?" Bertie had his doubts about trusting Ten Ends.

"He did try, shortly after he was brought here, but my husband Ralph was far too quick for him. Caught him before he'd got to the door and nipped his ankles. He hasn't bothered since."

Belinda, who by now had really warmed to Roxie Rat, asked if the ratlets would like a grooming before they settled down for the night, with the result that the two brushes spent the next half an hour stroking and pampering an excited clutch of small rodents, eager for some fuss and attention, while Cedric and Roxie caught up with the garden gossip.

With the morning fast approaching, Cedric reminded Belinda and Bertie of their mission.

"Come on, you two, time is running out. We must get going and see to the web traps. Time to say goodbye!"

Reluctantly, the toothbrushes bade their farewells and joined Cedric by the door, but not before Bertie, to the astonishment of Cedric and Belinda, ran across to Ten Ends, wished him good luck and asked him to take good care of the ratlets. "I hope it all works out for you, Ten Ends. Please look after Roxie for us. Perhaps we, too, might become friends."

The goblin, who was not used to such kindness, looked at Bertie awkwardly, nodded gently, and said very softly, "Thank you. That would be nice ... and I'll take good care of Roxie."

Belinda stopped briefly to wish Roxie all the best with the arrival of her new brood and, with that, the intrepid trio set off for the shed roof, with the plucky toothbrushes scaling the web ladders which Cedric had spun for them. In no time at all they were standing in the plastic gutter which ran along the side of the shed collecting water for the garden water butt. Cedric climbed out and under the gutter, gathering his harvest of flies, then handed them up to Bertie and Belinda ready to take back to his larder.

"Whooooosh!" Bertie was startled by a sudden rush of air immediately over his head and swung round to see a bird-like creature swooping around in the moonlight above him. The next moment it was diving again, this time straight at Bertie who ducked just in time, nearly falling out of the gutter as he did so.

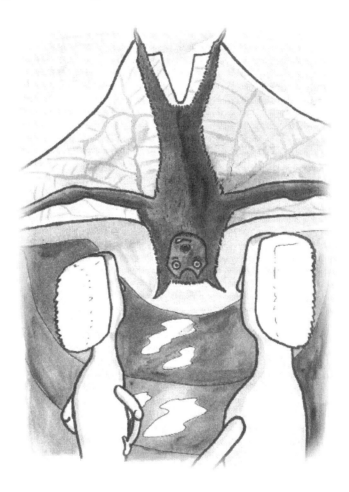

"What on earth is that?" Bertie shouted. Belinda, too, had stopped to look up at the speedy aerial acrobat whizzing around in the sky above them. Down it flew again, but this time it landed on the roof eave just above the channel in which they were standing, attached small hooks at the end of its wings on to the roof felt, then swung upside down into the gutter suspended by its wing tips. The two brushes bent upside down to look into its small mouse-like face just as Cedric appeared over the side of the gutter.

"Just what we need when we're busy," he groaned, "Scatty Batty!"

"Hi Cedric," Scatty squeaked. "Who are your friends? I've never seen anything like them. I had to do a double swoop to make sure that I wasn't seeing things."

Cedric introduced the toothbrushes to Scatty, explaining who they were and where they were from, while Scatty announced himself as Scatty Batty Bat-Robat.

Cedric whispered in Belinda's ear, "He's a bat, and he's barmy. Don't let him take you for a ride, whatever you do."

"You're an acrobat?" said Bertie who had developed quite a taste for flying after his trips with Sid Starling and Wye's Owl, "Would you take me for a spin?" and, before either Cedric or Belinda had had a chance to intervene, Bertie had leapt on Scatty's back and the two of them were shooting off into the night sky.

At first, Bertie was exhilarated to be soaring in the air with the wind whistling through his bristles. He remembered Bobby talking about a ride on a thing called a roller coaster and how thrilling it had been zooming up and down. This was even better! However, after 4 loop de loops, 3 vertical dives and a near miss with a chimney pot, Bertie began to wonder if this had been a good idea, especially as it felt that his tummy was being left behind. He was clinging on for dear life when Scatty decided to perform his stunt showpiece, flying upside-down inches above the ground, skimming across the lawn and over the pond.

It was on the second run that Bertie felt his grip loosening and his body sliding slowly down Scatty's back, until at last he could hold on no longer and dropped down right into the centre of the garden pond. He plunged under the surface, then floated back up

alongside a small crop of blue flag irises which he reached out and held on to.

"Nice of you to drop in!" croaked a friendly voice.

"I've been meaning to say thank you to you, Bertie, for rescuing Terence the other day." Ferdy Frog was sitting on his usual pondside stone but slipped into the water to bring Bertie back to the safety of the bank.

"I was watching your aerial acrobatics. You were either very brave or very stupid to take a ride with Scatty. He loves to show off and he has even won the prestigious Acorn Award for his flying stunts, but he definitely has a mad streak in him and completely ignores all the Health and Safety regulations. Anyway, what have you been up to?"

Bertie told Ferdy all about the fly collecting expedition, then suddenly realised that morning was approaching and that he'd need to get back to Cedric and Belinda. Freddie kindly obliged with a hopping lift across the lawn to the shed where the two parted company, with Bertie thanking Ferdy for his kindness. Up the web ladder, the small orange toothbrush was soon reunited with his two companions, although they had now been joined by a small company of bats, friends of Scatty, who had arrived to make amends for Scatty's rather reckless behaviour.

"We've come to fly you back to the roof," declared their spokesman, a rather distinguished looking bat who went by the name of Sir Vespers. "We're all loaded up with web sacks full of food for Cedric's larder. Hop on, you three … and Scatty, no antics, please."

The little flight of bats flew the travellers and their baggage the short journey back to the air vent on the roof. Cedric thanked them for their help, before they took their leave and whizzed off into the moonlit sky. Bertie and Belinda helped Cedric carry the fly bundles down the vent ladders and back to his larder. Then, after a quick goodbye, they set off through the pipes back to their bathroom home.

"What a night," exclaimed a very weary Bertie as he and his sister climbed back into their toothbrush rack, "Cats, rats and bats!"

SUNDAY NIGHT – A POND PARTY

Mr Evershed always liked to be in bed early on Sunday evening, reading a chapter of his book and enjoying a good night's rest before the hectic demands of Monday morning back at the office. By eleven he had dropped off to sleep and the house was calm and still. But presently, he was to have a very rude awakening …

In the meantime, just after eleven, Belinda and Bertie, the purple and orange toothbrushes belonging to the junior members of the Evershed family, Millie and Bobby, had arrived at Cedric the Spider's air vent home via the bath plug hole, then through a series of pipes in the plumbing at number 24, March Meadow.

Cedric greeted them with some excellent news. "Ah! Belinda, Bertie! Listen! We've all been invited to a party tonight at the garden pond. Ferdy Frog is throwing it for all his friends, old and new. He specifically asked me to let you two know. Ferdy's pond parties are legendary. Everyone who's anyone will be there. What's more, Sturnie, Sid and Shirley, the starlings, have offered to fly us out. We must climb up the vent to the roof again."

Bertie was so excited that he ran to the vertical pipe shaft to climb up the web ladder, but in his haste, slipped on a damp piece of floor pipe and, instead, fell down the shaft into the foul water stack below.

"Oh no!" cried Cedric in exasperation, "I'll have to go down and guide him through the smelly water pipes to the outside drain. He'll never find the way on his own. Belinda, you'll need to climb up the shaft to the roof and explain to Sturnie what has happened. We'll meet you all down below by the dustbins and walk to the pond together."

Accordingly, Cedric and Belinda parted company, with Belinda scaling the web ladder up to the air vent cap, then out on to the roof. She clambered up the tiles to Sturnie's nest on the ridge, where she found Sturnie cheerfully feeding his fledglings. She quickly explained what had happened and the friendly starling immediately agreed to fetch Sid and Shirley, and to fly down to the refuse bins.

Meanwhile, Cedric had found Bertie standing with his feet in a puddle of pongy water, at the bottom of the large vertical pipe known as the soil stack.

"Come to the edge, Bertie, and stand still while I climb on your head. I'll then lead us to the drain cover where there's a way out to the back garden."

With Cedric aloft and acting as guide, Bertie waded through the shallow foul water, along the sloping pipe until they reached the bottom of a manhole. Cedric looked up, climbed off Bertie's head, then shimmied up the wall, simultaneously spinning a web ladder for Bertie. In this way, they reached the underside of the manhole cover which, conveniently, had a small crack providing access to the patio outside the back door. The two of them squeezed through and out into the open air of the rear garden, then headed off towards the trellis-screened alcove which concealed the dustbins.

As they crossed the patio, Belinda flew in on Shirley Starling's back, dismounting to join them, with Sid and Sturnie landing alongside. However, before they were able to greet each other properly, they were interrupted by an almighty, but recognisable clatter - Kerraaash! Clunk! – coming from behind the screen. The three terrified starlings immediately took off and flew back to the safety of the roof, leaving Cedric, Bertie and Belinda to investigate.

The intrepid trio entered the alcove to witness a scene

of upturned bins, waste and devastation, at the centre of which a rather fat, black and white badger was stuffing himself with every bit of leftover food he could find.

"Boris, you idiot," Cedric shouted – although a spider shout is almost inaudible to the human ear – "You'll wake the whole household!" and, a moment later, they heard a key being turned in the back-door lock.

A very irate Mr Evershed emerged in his dressing gown and slippers, brandishing a long, folded umbrella with a sharp point on the end. Boris heard the human footsteps, turned, and fled down the garden, but not before he felt a sharp slap across his backside. Cedric quickly scuttled away, blending quietly into the trellis fencing, while Bertie and Belinda dived into the waste rubbish on the paving slabs and hid in some old newspapers.

It was now well after midnight, and Mr Evershed, tired, grumpy and eager to get back to bed as swiftly as possible, scooped up all the waste, stuffed it quickly back into the bins, replaced the lids and then put a couple of bricks on each bin as a protective deterrent against further raids. Bertie and Belinda were trapped inside!

Once the coast was clear and Mr Evershed had gone back to bed, Cedric assessed the situation and devised a plan to rescue the toothbrushes, although this would take some time to put into effect as it involved climbing the full length of the drainpipe up to the roof.

Nevertheless, after half an hour, he eventually reached Sturnie's nest, explained the situation, and accepted the starling's kind offer of a lift to Tanglewood to find Wye's Owl.

It didn't take Cedric long to convince Wye's Owl, or Mr Tawny as he liked to be called, of the need to rescue the two young toothbrushes. Furthermore, it was early on Monday morning that the men on the dust cart came to empty the bins, so there was no time to lose. In any case, they had to get Belinda and Bertie back to the house before the Eversheds rose in the morning, although there were still several hours to spare.

Mr Tawny sent Sturnie and Cedric back to the patio with instructions to find out in which of the two bins Bertie and Belinda were trapped. In the meantime, he went off to enlist some help.

Back at the patio, Sturnie used his beak to knock several times on the bins while Cedric clung closely to the side of each bin in turn to sense any vibration from within. The system was effective, and it wasn't long before Cedric both heard and felt a tapping coming from inside one of the two bins. Mr Tawny then flew in and was told the good news; they had located the two brushes. Shortly afterwards, Boris Badger came huffing and puffing around the corner, having had an ear-bashing from Wye's Owl for his stupidity, and orders to knock the bricks off the bin lid.

"The only problem," said Mr Tawny, scratching his head, "is how to prevent the bricks making a lot of noise as they fall to the ground."

"I think I can solve that one," Sturnie declared. "Just give me five minutes …"

He flew off immediately, with the others gazing after him wondering what on earth he was up to. Very soon he returned, however, after which everything became clear.

"He's brought the murmuration!" Cedric cried, and the others looked up in amazement as at least a thousand starlings were swirling around above them, all in close formation behind Sturnie. They created spectacular, shifting shapes in the night sky before swooping down to the patio in distinct order, each dropping a leaf in a spot next to the bin where Bertie and Belinda were trapped.

"Well done, Sturnie!" hooted Wye's Owl as the starling flew down from the flock to join his friends. As Mr Tawny was not known to dispense praise without very good reason, Sturnie felt a flutter of pride inside his feathery chest.

"Right ho! Get on with it, Boris, push those bricks off on to the leaf pile and …" Wye's Owl stared menacingly into the badger's eyes, "DO IT QUIETLY!!"

Obediently, Boris stood up on his rear legs and used his front paws to heave the two bricks on to the cushion of leaves below. Immediately the great owl flapped his mighty wings and flew upwards until he hovered over the dustbin, then, grabbing the handle of the bin lid in his powerful claws, he lifted it and carried it away a few wing spans, before lowering it gently on to the garden lawn.

Boris stretched up again to look down into the bin, just as two happy and relieved faces appeared over the rim and gazed back at him.

"Come on, you two," the badger beamed, "Let me lift you out of there."

After a journey through the sewer pipe and a stopover in

the dustbin, Bertie was not exactly smelling of roses, and the others tried desperately not to express their revulsion as the whiff caused their noses to twitch and their eyes to water.

Belinda, however, was less polite. "Good gracious, Bertie, you stink! You'd better get down to that pond immediately and have a good bath."

While Bertie and Belinda set off down the garden path towards the pond, Mr Tawny replaced the dustbin lid and flapped his wings to scatter the leaves. Boris did his best to lift the bricks back on to the lid, but they were too heavy, even for him, and the bricks had to be left on the ground. When all was done, Cedric, Boris, Sturnie and Wye's Owl all followed the toothbrushes down the path. The pond party would soon be under way.

The pond was located behind a long box hedge and was, therefore, conveniently situated for the party-goers, as they could not be seen from the house. It was surrounded by an attractive mixture of paving stones, pebble beaches and marginal water plants, always eye-catching in the daytime, but on this night it was quite spectacular.

As Bertie and Belinda arrived, they marvelled at the scene before them. A large ring of glow worms surrounded the water's edge, affording a magical half-light, which reflected enchantingly in the pond itself ...

Cedric had asked Lux and Lumen, his glow worm, 'lightbulb' lodgers, to bring their friends along. The glimmering creatures were chatting among themselves in Larvin as they renewed friendships: "So, so, so; like so; like, so!" Only *they* knew what they were talking about.

The young toothbrushes quickly recognised many of their new friends and were eager to say hello; Nigella Newt, smooth, but most definitely not common; Shirley and Sid Starling, who had flown back down from the roof; Roxie and Ralph Rat with a small cluster of ratlets, although the latest brood had not yet arrived. More surprisingly, a couple of the smaller rats were playing tag with their new 'uncle', Ten Ends the doctor goblin, who seemed very much to be enjoying his new role in life. Bertie waved to him and he smiled amiably back. Locum, having recovered from his recent ordeal in Tanglewood, was also there and eager to thank Belinda and Bertie for their part in his rescue, although his sensitive medical skills quickly homed in on the smell emanating from Bertie.

"Bertie, you're either suffering from advanced toothbrush decay or you need a jolly good bath! Get in that pond immediately!"

"Hear! Hear!" Mr Tawny, Cedric, Sturnie and Boris had just arrived and watched with merriment as Locum grabbed hold of Bertie by the bristles and pushed him off the bank and into the water, an event which prompted laughter all around the pond. "Like," said Lux, "Like," said Lumen.

Finally, their host, Ferdy Frog, sitting on his favourite pebble, called everyone to order, welcomed the assembled gathering and thanked them all for coming, at which he received a hearty round of applause. The party had begun.

Ferdy's wife, Freda, served fruity drinks, blackberry and elderberry juice in acorn cups. She was ably assisted by some of her older tadpoles, one of which Belinda recognised as Terence, who had now sprouted a small set of legs. Mavis Thrush and Gail Nightingale, a talented musical duet, entertained the guests with some beautiful, pastoral melodies, and it wasn't long before everyone who knew the birdsongs joined in.

In the pond, some of the ratlets and a small nest of mice were enjoying lily pad raft rides, propelled along by Nigella and some of her newt friends and relations. Once Bertie had had a thorough wash, he too jumped on a raft and waved to his friends on the bank.

Everyone was enjoying the party to the full, the music, the illuminations, the drinks and the rides, when suddenly Wye's Owl screeched out loud and they all fell silent. He then delivered a very long hoot, looked up and raised his great wings skywards. The aerial display had started!

It began with a dazzling demonstration of acrobatics from Scatty Batty and his Bat-Robats; breath-taking swoops, daring loop de loops, high speed dives and precision pond skimming, every move eliciting 'Oooohs' and 'Aaaahs' from the audience below. Wye's Owl himself then soared up into the air, stalled, and hovered directly above the pond. He hooted loudly again, "Tu whit tu whoooooo!" and instantly the sky was filled with thousands of starlings, a magnificent, mesmerising murmuration, which, after creating a dozen or so spectacular moving shapes in the sky, flew around Mr Tawny to form a huge owl silhouette, with the owl himself forming the central feature, the hooked, aquiline beak, an absolutely stunning finale!

Cheers and applause came from below as the display concluded and Cedric at last looked around to find Bertie and Belinda in order to take them home. He found them at the pond's edge talking to Ferdy, thanking him and Freda for such a wonderful party. Cedric waited until they had finished and then announced, "Belinda and Bertie, I have one more surprise for you before we return home. Face the pond and close your eyes!"

The curious brushes did as they were told, wondering what on earth Cedric had in store for them.

After a brief pause and some scuffling sounds, Cedric commanded "Now, open your eyes!"

They again obeyed, looked up, and gasped in surprise at the sight in front of them. All their friends were standing there on the pond's edge waving and clapping, but most startling of all, Mr and Mrs Brush, their parents, were at the front smiling back at them.

Mr Brush spoke first: "Well, you two, you've certainly given us a few scares this week with all the scrapes you've found yourselves in, but, with Cedric's help and the support of all your friends here, your mother and I are pleased that you've learned so much, that you've been resourceful, and, at the same time, have always tried to be kind and helpful to others. Ferdy was so grateful to you for helping Terence that he held this party in your honour. We'd like to thank him very much and, also, all you other good friends here. But most of all, we would like to thank the one companion who we asked specially to keep an eye on you both, Cedric Aloysius Octopod, better known to you all as Cedric the Spider."

Cedric looked very embarrassed as Bertie bent down and put the little spider on his head, to the cheers and applause of all present. Then Cedric himself asked for silence and spoke quietly to the gathering: "It's been a pleasure looking after Bertie and Belinda, but I must admit, it's been such a busy seven days, I'm quite exhausted. I'd very much like to put my feet up now, but I don't have eight stools!" Everyone chuckled. "Perhaps I'll get a bit of peace and quiet back home next week ..."

Mr and Mrs Brush and Belinda bristled in agreement.

Bertie muttered quietly to himself "... and perhaps not!"

THE END

ABOUT THIS BOOK

I dreamt up Cedric, Bertie and Belinda years ago as bedtime stories for my children and, more recently, for my grandchildren. The initial intention was to prevent them from being afraid of spiders and to encourage them to clean their teeth. A more subliminal purpose was to develop in them a love for the natural world.

I made up the stories as I went along, never myself quite knowing what was going to happen next. Strangely the same feeling still sweeps over me today as I attempt to set them down on paper. It constantly surprises me when another idea suddenly springs to mind, and another surreal event transpires.

The book consists of seven, 15-20 minute bedtime stories, one for each day of the week. Older children will read them for themselves, parents will read them to the younger ones. The daily dose will encourage children to want another story, but will, eponymously, allow parents to postpone such requests until the following evening.

The stories focus on the adventures of Cedric the Spider and two children's toothbrushes, Belinda and Bertie, who meet when Cedric emerges from the bath plug hole in the bathroom.

It was in June 2018, just after my 72nd birthday, that my daughter, Emily, asked me to write the stories down. My preferred literary output had hitherto been poetry, sometimes romantic, sometimes cautionary, but more commonly around celebratory events, such as births, marriages or vocational farewells. Poetry provided structure and encouraged economy of thought, whereas prose knew no boundaries and led Cedric, Belinda, Bertie and me blindly into the unknown ...

Jack Webb is a pseudonym. The author lives in Suffolk.

Printed in Great Britain
by Amazon